THE COOL M

Heroic deeds of Finn Mac Coc

The ancient legends of Finn Mac Cool
once handed down by oral tradition
now in comic verse and zany drawings

The tale of Finn's favourite hounds — Bran and Sceolan — half dog, half human!
The Salmon of Knowledge, who tempts the Poet, but ends up on Finn's plate.
The Fire-Fiend, who threatens to burn down Tara's halls, but has to reckon with Finn's skill and daring.

Entertaining — amusing — informative

GORDON SNELL

Author, dramatist, song-writer. Publications include: *The Book of Theatre Quotes*, *The King of Quizzical Island*, *Tom's Amazing Machine*. Scripted a series on Kerry for Channel Four, and has broadcast extensively on BBC radio and television. He is one of the scriptwriters on RTE's comic series *Only Slaggin'*

WENDY SHEA

Illustrator, painter and theatre designer. Creator of the popular strip cartoon O'Brien, in the *Sunday Tribune*. Head of design at the Abbey Theatre for nine years. Lectures in theatre design at Trinity College Dublin, and also exhibits her own painting.

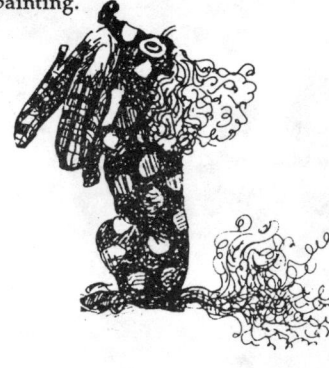

First published 1988 by
The O'Brien Press 20 Victoria Road,
Rathgar, Dublin 6, Ireland.
Copyright © text Gordon Snell,
Illustrations © Wendy Shea

All rights reserved. No part of this book may be
reproduced or utilised in any form or by any
means, electronic or mechanical, including
photocopying, recording or by any
information storage and retrieval
system without permission in writing
from the publisher. This book
may not be sold as a remainder,
bargain book, or at a reduced
price without written
permission from
the publisher.

*British Library Cataloguing
in Publication Data*
Snell, Gordon.
The cool Mac Cool.
1. Children's: humorous
   poetry in English, 1945--.
I. Title II. Shea, Wendy.
821'.914
ISBN 0-86278-176-0

Book Design:
Michael O'Brien
Typeset at
The O'Brien Press
Printing:
Guernsey Press
Co. Ltd.,
Channel Islands

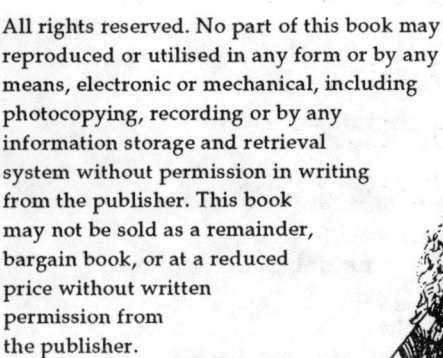

THE
COOL Mac COOL

Heroic Deeds of Finn Mac Cool Legendary Celtic Hero

Words
GORDON SNELL

Drawings
WENDY SHEA

THE O'BRIEN PRESS
DUBLIN

About These Stories

Finn Mac Cool has certainly got the secret of long life: he has been a hero for over fifteen hundred years — more than a millennium and a half.

Even before the Irish language was written down at all, people were telling tales about the deeds of Finn, and he has continued to be one of the most popular characters in Ireland's poems and stories right down to our own time.

Before modern communications, Finn and his band of warriors had the same kind of appeal as characters in a favourite TV series do today, and people were eager to hear more and more about his adventures in the strange legendary world full of fierce battles, heroism, treachery, magical creatures and amazing sporting feats.

The way the stories were told over the centuries ranged from stern and tragic to comic and light-hearted. The versions in this book are very much on the light-hearted side of the tradition, but the plots themselves are the same as those which storytellers have been using for hundreds of years.

So here, treated from a modern humorous point of view, are the great characters of three of the Finn stories: the devilish Fire-Fiend, the furious Fairy who turns people into hounds, and the amazing Salmon which gives Finn his power of knowledge — and of course, the greatest character of all, Finn himself, the hero who shows how well he deserves the name, the Cool Mac Cool.

Contents

Finn and His Favourite Hounds
page 7

Finn and the Salmon of Knowledge
page 32

Finn and the Fire-Fiend
page 53

*For Maeve and Séamus
with much love*

Finn and His Favourite Hounds

Finn had a hundred hounds or more
To help him hunt the deer and boar,
But Bran and Sceolan were the best:
He loved them more than all the rest.

The Dog Show judges were agreed —
That pair were very rare indeed.
And here is how it all began,
This tale of Sceolan and of Bran.

THE VISIT

One day, Finn's mother called on him;
She said: 'Now, son, I just dropped in
So that my sister here can view
Your handsome, hunky warrior crew.

'Now don't forget, she's very choosy,
Hates men who're bloated, bald or boozy,
And yet among your lot she might
Discover lucky Mister Right!

The man she picks will be in clover —
So why not let her look them over?'

THE AUNT

Tuiren, Finn's aunt, was young and fair:
All smooth and shiny was her hair.
Her eyes seemed deeper than a lake,
Her voice like music angels make.

Oh, how the warriors' hearts were stirred!
They muttered: 'What a smashing bird!'
And other chivalrous remarks,
And smiled at her like hungry sharks.

But Finn said: 'Hold it! That's enough
Of all this lovey-dovey stuff.
So cut the nudges and the winks:
Let Tuiren tell us what she thinks —
But I'll be most surprised, it's true,
If she should fancy one of you!'

THE HUSBAND

But Tuiren blushed, and then confessed:
'There's one I like above the rest —
That fellow there is quite a dish,
The answer to a maiden's wish,
And I would like to ask him whether
He thinks we two might get together.'

She stepped towards Iollan, who replied:
'Fair Tuiren, if you'll be my bride,
I'll be the happiest of men.'
So Finn said: 'Well, that's settled, then —
This very day she'll be your wife.
You'll swear to love her all your life,
For if you don't, or won't, or can't,
I'll never let you wed my aunt!'

So Iollan swore it, there and then —
Which goes to show, you can't trust men:
For Tuiren later would discover
That Iollan had a *secret lover*.

THE LOVER

Her name was Uct Dealv — Fair of Breast —
She'd travelled north, south, east and west,
And men had loved her, everywhere,
But none with Iollan could compare.
She found him cuddlier and cuter
Than any other love-lorn suitor.

From Fairyland this lady came,
And truly, she was quite a dame!
They met at night, in fairy raths,
And wandered down the moonlit paths
Where leafy branches arched above,
And there they whispered words of love.

When news of Iollan's marriage came,
Her rage boiled up like seas of flame:
She screamed and swore, and changed her shape,
First to a huge and hairy ape,
Then to a beetle, then a bat,
A crab, a cockroach and a cat!

It's by this kind of transformation
That fairies show their irritation.

She said: 'I've got a funny feeling
That he'll regret his double-dealing!
Now I've discovered what he's at,
I'll be revenged upon the rat.

'I'll be revenged on *her* as well —
I've got the most enchanting spell.
Finn's messenger I'll seem to be:
She'll curse the day she challenged *me!*'

THE 'MESSENGER'

She called on Iollan's wife next day,
Knowing her husband was away.
'You are a messenger from Finn?'
Said Tuiren, 'Well then, please come in.'

Uct Dealv, her eyes a-glow with hate,
Replied: 'I can't, it's getting late.
If you will walk a little way,
I'll tell you what I've got to say.'

She led her off, among the trees:
Tuiren was feeling ill at ease.
She said: 'The message — tell it me:
I must go home and get the tea.'

The Fairy laughed a laugh so shrill,
Even the hedgehogs' blood grew chill.
She shrieked: 'There'll be no tea for you!
When I've done what I mean to do
You will be happy with a crust —
So now, take that, and bite the dust!'

THE SPELL

She took her magic rod and gave
A weird and wild and witch-like wave,
Then tapped it hard on Tuiren's head,
And Tuiren seemed to fall down dead.

But soon she woke again, and found
That she'd been changed into a hound.
She raised her head and tried to shout,
But only yaps and barks came out.

She raised her hand towards her head
And found it was a paw instead.
She tried to stand, and then she knew
She'd got four legs, instead of two!

The Fairy said: 'Now, don't you fret —
You really are a little pet.
I'll tell you what we're going to do:
We'll find a lovely home for you.'

THE DOG-HATER!

She led the hound for miles, until
They reached a house upon a hill.
She told her: 'Fergus owns this house,
And if you were a loathsome louse
He'd be more pleased to see you here
Than when he sees a *dog* appear.
He hates all dogs with much more anger
Than anyone, from Bray to Bangor.'

The poor hound trembled in despair
When Fergus saw her standing there.
He shook his fist and gave a frown,
And started jumping up and down.

He shouted: 'Take away that cur!
I cannot stand the sight of her!
I hate all dogs, from chow to spaniel,
Just as the lions hated Daniel.

'I hate their barks, their growls, their licks,
I hate their silly little tricks,
I hate the way they run for sticks,
The way they pant, and drool, and sweat,
And leave the lamp-posts soaking wet!'

The Fairy said: 'Stop, Fergus dear —
I'll have you know, Finn sent her here.
He wants her minded for a while,
So take her, Fergus, with a smile!'

She pushed the dog in through the door,
And said: 'Farewell, for ever more!'
She laughed and ran off, hell for leather,
Leaving the two of
 them together.

The little dog was all a-quiver,
But Fergus growled: 'Oh, please don't shiver!
If you're Finn's hound, I'll never strike you.
Just don't expect I'll ever like you!'

THE PUPPIES

But soon the grumbling Fergus found
He liked to have the dog around.
He'd pat her head, and take her walking,
And she would listen to him talking.

He was amazed to find, one day,
That by her side, two puppies lay —
And he, who once thought dogs so frightful,
Found these two creatures quite delightful.

THE THREAT

Finding his wife had disappeared,
Iollan went wild and chewed his beard,
And roared: 'Who's done this deed to me?'
But he knew well who it must be.
His spirits sank, his face was grim,
When Finn, his leader, summoned him.

'Iollan, you give me great distress —
To lose your wife is carelessness!
She is my aunt, most dear to me,
And harshly punished you shall be.

'Sharp spikes shall be your dungeon bed,
While slime drips down upon your head,
And bugs and beetles make you thinner
By taking bites of you for dinner!'

Then Iollan fell upon his knees
And cried: 'Oh Finn, have mercy, please!
Give me one day to find her first —
And if I can't, then do your worst!'

THE BARGAIN

'Okay,' said Finn, and Iollan then
Sought out his lover in the glen.
He begged for pity in his plight,
But she replied: 'It serves you right!
You married someone else. How dare you?
And yet — I could get Finn to spare you.
To human form I'll change your wife,
If you will then be mine for life.'

'I will!' he cried, with eager voice —
He really hadn't got much choice.

THE ANTI-SPELL

When Fergus opened up his door,
There stood Finn's messenger once more.
She said: 'I've come to fetch the hound —
I hope you kept it safe and sound.'

'I did,' he said, 'and as you see,
You brought one hound, and now there's three!'
The Fairy stared, and thought: 'Well, well!
This needs a *very* powerful spell!'

The three dogs didn't want to leave,
And parting made poor Fergus grieve.
He patted them with fond goodbyes,
And tears of sadness in his eyes.

The Fairy led them to a wood
And said: 'I don't like doing good,
But now I've got to change you back.'
She gave the hound a hefty whack,
And said a spell, and then and there
She turned into a lady fair.

The Fairy whacked each little pup
And snarled: 'Now children, you stand up!'
The puppies stared — they heard her call,
And yet they didn't change at all!

She stormed about, and waved her stick,
And went through every magic trick,
But those two pups could not obey:
Hounds they were born and hounds they'd stay.

The Fairy said: 'I've no regrets —
I get the man, you get the pets.
At least they'll keep you company,
Now Iollan's coming back to *me*!'

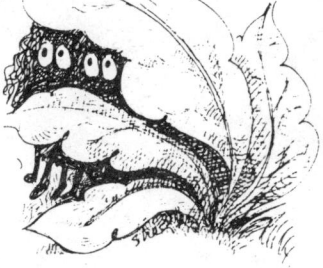

She vanished then without a sound,
And Tuiren sadly stroked each hound.
They wagged their tails and licked her hand —
She thought they seemed to understand.

She brought them home — Finn's joy was great.
He said: 'Let's feast and celebrate;
And bring the hounds into the Hall —
They're my relations, after all!'

Iollan was banished in disgrace,
And went to live in that strange place
Where magic rules, and fairies dwell,
And humans don't get on too well.
Uct Dealv would boss him, day and night —
And truth to tell, it served him right.

THE PET HOUNDS

The hounds became Finn's joy and pride,
And they were always at his side.

Their bowls were lined with precious stones
And filled with all the juiciest bones.
They slept on cushions made of silk,
And washed their paws in tiger's milk.

They grew up very bright indeed:
Finn even taught them both to read.
When music played, then very soon
The hounds joined in, and barked the tune.

No wonder strangers' eyes were wide
When Finn, the two hounds by his side,
Would tell them how it all began,
This tale of Sceolan and of Bran.

Finn and the
Salmon of Knowledge

Long ago, beneath the sea,
There grew a magic hazel-tree.
Its nuts, enchanted by a spell,
Had Knowledge hidden in the shell.
The tree stood very near a well,
And there a Salmon used to dwell.

He didn't need to go to school,
For when the nuts fell in the pool
He ate them up, and said with glee:
'I really fancy nuts for tea —
And thanks to all those tasty dishes
I'm now the brainiest of fishes!'

THE TRAVELLER

From time to time, the fish would make
A journey to a distant lake:
Across the oceans he would go
To lands where mighty rivers flow.
He liked a change, for truth to tell,
It's boring, living in a well.

Now on the way, he'd stop and chat
To other fish, of this and that:
He'd talk of party politics,
And then he'd do some conjuring tricks,
And speak, with many growls and grunts,
In several languages at once.

The highest marks were always his
In every general knowledge quiz.
The angry losers used to scoff:
'That Salmon's always showing off!'

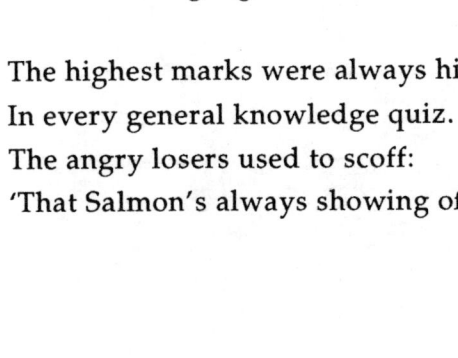

But rumours of the things he knew
Spread far and wide, as rumours do:
Some shoals of soles were even bent
On making him the President!

THE POET

A Poet also heard the rumour —
It put him in the best of humour.
He'd catch that Salmon in his net,
And then, what Knowledge he would get!

He'd eat it all, skin, bone and scale,
The head, the eyes, the fins, the tail.
Roasted or toasted, fried or stewed,
He longed to gulp that fishy food.
He'd be as wise as wise could be,
If he could have that fish for tea.

Finegas was the poet's name —
To everybody he'd proclaim:
'I am the best and brightest bard
From Aughnacloy to Oughterard!'

Beside the Boyne he made his camp —
He didn't care about the damp.
It was his one and only wish
To dine upon that Know-All Fish.

He said: 'To help me in my mission,
I'll hold a Knowledge Competition.
Whichever fish can show he's wise
Will get a very big surprise —
For I'll invite the lucky winner
To join me in a slap-up dinner!'

Fish came and went between the banks,
But they were all as thick as planks.
Although they swam around in schools,
They gaped and gawped like perfect fools.

FINN ARRIVES

For seven years time seemed to crawl,
And still that Salmon didn't call.
The Poet got a bit depressed
Until one day he had a guest:
'My name,' he said, 'is Finn Mac Cool,
And I would like to go to school
And learn to be a proper poet.
If there's a way, I'm sure you know it.'

Finegas shook him by the hand:
'I am the finest in the land.
If poetry is your delight,
I'll teach you how to write it right!'

And so Finn stayed and studied hard
To learn the secrets of the Bard.
One day, he looked into the river
And saw a sight that made him quiver:
A silver Salmon, huge and proud,
Was talking to himself out loud!

The Salmon said: 'Now once again
It's time to exercise my brain.
I'll put my mind to mathematics
And do some mental acrobatics.
I might design a new computer,
Or else a supersonic scooter.'

Finn listened, then began to shout:
'That's what I'll write an ode about!
To find a real live talking Salmon
Is like being given bread with jam on!
Perhaps I'll join him for a swim:
I'd really learn a lot from *him*!'

Finegas heard his cries of joy.
He said: 'That Salmon's mine, my boy!
I've waited seven years to meet it —
And now at last I'm going to eat it!
This river bank will be the venue:
Don't write an ode, just write the menu!'

THE PRIZE

Then with his net Finegas lunged:
He tripped and fell, and down he plunged!
Well might the Poet fume and fret —
He'd fallen straight into his net!

The Salmon told him, with a grin:
'You're welcome — thanks for dropping in!
I've got no whiskey, beer or porter,
But won't you take a drink of water?'

Finn hauled the dripping Poet out;
They heard the laughing Salmon shout:
'It's nice to meet you, come back soon —
We'll tell a tale and play a tune,
And drink a muddy glass or two,
And eat a dish of may-fly stew.'

The cunning Bard said: 'Salmon dear,
From what you say, it's very clear
That you're the wisest fish around.'
'If any wiser can be found,'
The Salmon said, 'then I'm a clam!
A genius is what I am —
My brain's the most enormous size.'
'Then,' said the Bard, 'you get the prize!'

The Salmon said: 'A prize, no less!
What can it be? Now let me guess.
A bowl of worms? A cup? A shield?
A holiday in Sellafield?

'A silver polish for my scales,
A record of the Singing Whales,
A spotted sea-horse for a pet,
A fishing-hook removal set...?'

The Poet said, with hungry eyes:
'It is a Bumper Mystery Prize.
You wonder now, what *can* it be?
Then come up here, and you will see!'

THE CATCH

The Salmon knew the risk he took
In popping up to take a look —
For though he boasted many skills,
The air just didn't suit his gills.

He needed, to survive in it,
Some kind of fresh-air diver's kit,
So he could go and live a while
Upon the land, in human style.
For after all, those men and women
Used *his* world as a place to swim in;
Some even came and gazed like trippers,
In idiotic masks and flippers.

The Bard said: 'Come and take a peep —
It only needs a little leap.
We'll shake your fin, and say Hello;
You take the prize, and back you go!'

The fish could not resist the bait —
His curiosity was great.
He flicked his tail and made the jump,
And landed with a squishy bump.

The Poet shook his fin in greeting
And said: 'Oh, what a pleasant meeting —
I hope you'll stay a little while?'
'Living on air is not my style,'
The Salmon said, with watery eyes.
'So if you please, I'll take the prize.'

The Poet raised the fishing net
And bellowed: 'Here's the prize you get!'
He brought it down — the fish was caught.
The Salmon knew his time was short,
And yet he felt no twinge of fear.
He sensed that Fate had brought him here
So he could pass his Knowledge on
To someone else, when he was gone.

THE FISH'S FAREWELL

Finn was the man, the Salmon knew,
That he would pass his Knowledge to.
He saw his future, great and grand —
He saw him lead a warrior band
In battles grisly, grim and gory,
And spur them on to deeds of glory.

He smiled and said: 'You silly Poet!
You've lost the prize, and do not know it,

And now you've got a shock in store:
You'll stay as foolish as before,
However many tricks you try.
It's time for me to say goodbye.
My work is done, my time has passed.'
He smiled at Finn, and breathed his last.

The Poet said: 'I've never heard
A speech so fishy and absurd —
I really don't believe a word.'

Finn said: 'He was a wondrous creature —
He knew much more than any teacher,
Or quiz-show host, or telly-preacher!'

'Yes,' said the Bard, 'and when I'm fed,
His Knowledge will be mine instead.
My wisdom will the world amaze:
Finn, go and mix the mayonnaise!'

'I'll do exactly as you wish,'
Said Finn, 'but first I'll cook the fish —
Unless you want to eat it raw?'
'I'd rather eat a vulture's claw!'
The Poet snapped. 'Yes, cook it, do —
But bear in mind, there's none for you!'

THE MEAL

Finn heated up the frying pan —
The giant Salmon soon began
To sizzle with a luscious smell,
And cast an aromatic spell.

As Finn leaned down, and breathed it in,
He saw a blister on the skin.
It swelled up just like bubble-gum —
Finn pressed it downward with his thumb.

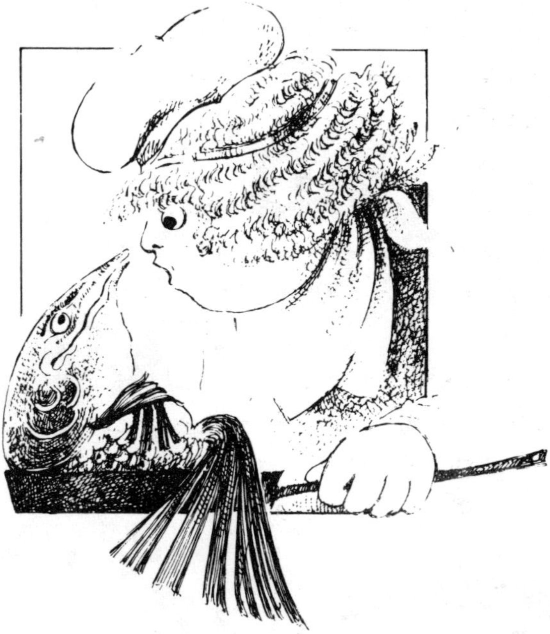

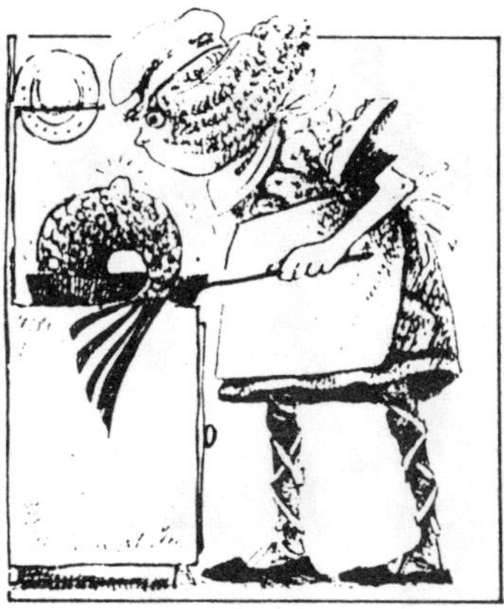

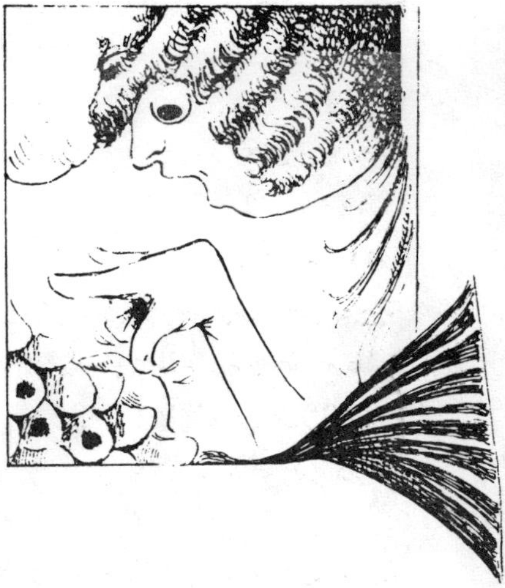

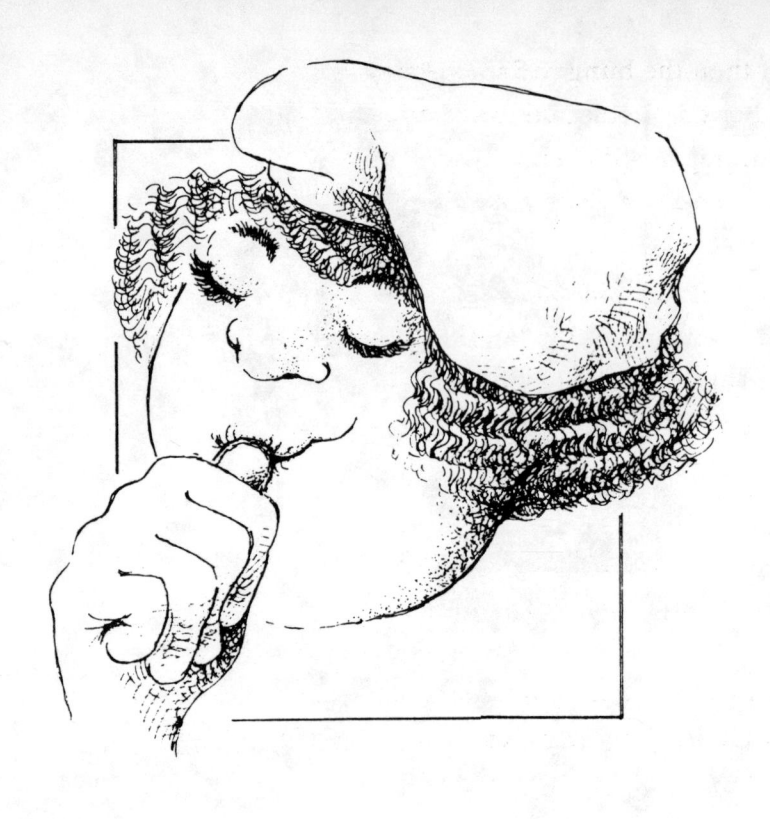

He licked the thumb to make it cool,
And thereby broke the Poet's rule.
His head at once began to swim:
He knew the fish was meant for *him*!

Just then the hungry Bard returned
And cried: 'Look out! It's nearly burned!
Finn, put the Salmon on the plate —
That fish and I have got a date.'

Finn took the plate and set it down,
And then he saw the Poet frown;
He grumbled, as he licked his lips:
'I wish you'd thought of making chips!'

He looked at Finn and said: 'You seem
As if you're living in a dream —
A very happy dream, as well.'
'The truth,' said Finn, 'I've got to tell.
The facts, though fishy, must be faced —
I had a teeny-weeny taste.'

The Poet shouted, turning white:
'You mean you went and took a bite?'
'No, no, I simply licked my thumb.'
'Curses! How *could* you be so dumb?'
The Bard was weeping: 'Now, I'll never
Be extra-wise, and ultra-clever!'

'Why not?' said Finn, 'the fish is there.'
The Bard said: 'No, the Fates declare
Whoever tastes it, eats it all,
And after that, he's walking tall —
He gets the Salmon's Knowledge, too.
It seems that it was meant for *you*.

'Now seven years have gone to waste,
And I won't even get a taste!
So sit right down, and eat your dinner
While I just stand here, getting thinner!'

Finn sat and did as he was told —
He couldn't let the meal get cold.
That hungry hero ate and ate,
Till there was nothing on the plate.
The Poet watched him eat it all,
And dribbled like a waterfall.

Then Finn sat back, and sucked his thumb,
And saw the shape of things to come:
A glorious vision was revealed
Of triumph on the battlefield.
He'd lead the Fianna forth to glory —
A hero, hailed in Ireland's story.

He smiled, and told the hungry Bard:
'I know it must be very hard
To hang around for seven years
Until your chosen meal appears.
No wonder you were looking nervous —
That's not exactly fast-food service!'

The Bard replied: 'It wasn't fun —
But after all, what's done is done.
I won't resort to oaths and curses,
I'll just go back to writing verses.'

THE TOAST

Then Finn said: 'Now, instead of salmon,
I'll cook you cabbages and gammon,
With apple pie and cream to follow.'
'Now there's a feast I'll gladly swallow,'
The Poet said. 'There's wine here too,
So I shall drink a toast to you
To wish you luck in your career —
And don't forget, it started here.'

'I won't forget,' said Finn, 'You'll see,
For well-rewarded you shall be.
I hold you in such high esteem,
I want to have you on my team —
For you're the Bard that Ireland needs
To sing about the Fianna's deeds.'

They filled their glasses, raised them high,
And Finn said: 'Let us say goodbye
To that great fish which paid the price,
And made the final sacrifice —
And also tasted very nice!

'The quest for Knowledge never ends —
So let us drink to Absent Friends!'

Finn and the Fire-Fiend

'Don't play with fire!' young Finn was told —
'It's better to be blue with cold.
It really isn't very bright
To go and set yourself alight!
So mind you keep that golden rule,
And earn your name — The Cool Mac Cool.'

So Finn grew up, avoiding games
With matches, fires, and candle-flames;
His birthday cakes were quite a sight,
Lit only by the glow-worms' light.

But one day Finn was forced to go
And fight against a fiery foe —
A Fiend whose one and only craze
Was setting everything ablaze.

TARA'S HALLS

It happened when he went to call
Upon the High King in his hall.
Each year the King would hold a feast
That lasted for a week at least;
Finn thought he'd join the celebration,
Although he had no invitation.

The King had all the Fianna there —
His warrior band, of courage rare:
And when it came to hearty eating,
That greedy crew would take some beating.

Finn watched Commander Goll, their chief,
Demolishing a joint of beef:
He gulped it down in one big swallow,
With half a ton of spuds to follow;
And then he ate a leg of pork,
Three larks, six turkeys and a stork.
The belch he uttered after that
Knocked half a dozen warriors flat.

Goll caught Finn's eye, and growled: 'It's rude
To stare at someone else's food.
I've never seen you here before —
Whoever let you in the door?'

He lunged at Finn, who struggled clear
And leaped upon the chandelier.
Its candles — and it had a lot! —
Were making Finn feel very hot.

Goll raised his spear — Finn gave a bound,
And tumbled down towards the ground.
He landed with a gruesome groan
Right there before the High King's throne.

The King said: 'That was quite a bump —
But boy, you sure know how to jump!
You could be useful, it would seem,
In Ireland's next Olympic team.
You're clearly an athletics star,
But kindly tell us who you are.'

Finn told the King, who said: 'My lad,
You're welcome here — I knew your Dad.
So Goll, just put away your spear,
And give young Finn a pint of beer.'

The plates were filled, the liquor flowed —
Finn feared that they would all explode.
He wondered how this warrior band
Could duel, or fight, or even stand!
So he was startled when the King
Said: 'Now it's time to dance and sing!'

Though Goll was fatter than a pig,
He staggered up, and danced a jig.
The sweat poured off him, more and more,
And made a pool upon the floor.

Another warrior was able
To do a step-dance on the table —
But then they saw him slip and stumble,
And fall into the apple crumble.

On went the *céilí*, full of joy —
They sang 'The Banks' and 'Danny Boy',
Then Goll began to spoil the party
By demonstrating his karate.
But when the seventh warrior fell,
The King stood up,
   and rang a bell.

He cried: 'It's time to stop the fun —
There's something now that must be done.
Tonight's the night when, every year,
The dreaded Fire-Fiend will appear.

THE FIEND

'Aillen will come, with harp in hand,
And use the tricks of Fairyland:
His music sends us all to sleep,
And while we lie in slumber deep
That Fiend of Fire will go to town,
And burn this noble hall right down!
He has, we really must conclude,
A most unfriendly attitude.'

Goll shouted: 'This has got to stop:
I'll serve him a karate chop!'

'You said that last year,' smiled the King,
'But when he plucked the magic string
You crashed right down upon the floor
And straight away began to snore.'

'There's got to be a way,' said Finn
'To fight this fearful Fiend, and win!'

'Well, if there is,' the King said sadly,
'I'd pay a fortune for it, gladly —
I fear the problem can't be cured.
At least the place is well insured!

'And on the night the hall is fired,
Hot-water bottles aren't required;
But, so the fiery flames won't harm us,
We all put on fire-proof pyjamas.'

FINN'S PLOT

Finn sucked his thumb — the knowledge came:
Now he could save them from the flame!
He asked the King how long they'd got.
'He comes at midnight, on the dot,'
The King replied, 'he'll play his tune,
And we'll be dozing very soon.'

Finn said: 'My Lord, it's half past ten —
By midnight I'll be back again,
And I shall bring what you desire:
A way to beat that Fiend of Fire!'

The King said: 'Finn, if you succeed,
Then I'll reward your glorious deed.'
Goll growled: 'His boasts aren't
   worth a damn!'
And swallowed down a leg of lamb.

THE SECRET WEAPON

Finn ran so fast, I do declare,
He even overtook a hare.
He'd sucked his thumb, and he could see
A man called Fiacha held the key —
The magic secret that would bring
Triumph to Finn, and to his King.

Fiacha said: 'Why, yes indeed,
I've got the very thing you need —
But who has told you where to come?'
Finn simply smiled, and sucked his thumb.

Fiacha thought: 'Who *is* this bloke?
Perhaps it's all a silly joke;
Yet, if it's true, then I can see
There could be riches here for *me*!'

He said to Finn: 'If you agree
To share the King's reward with me,
My secret weapon I'll reveal.'
Finn quickly answered: 'It's a deal!'

Then Fiacha took a rusty spear
And said: 'I have the weapon here.'

Finn scoffed: 'That spear! Oh, have a heart —
I wouldn't use it as a dart!
I'll have you know, I'm not a fool,
I'm Fearless Finn, The Cool Mac Cool!'

The man replied: 'Well, suit yourself —
I'll put it back upon the shelf.
I spoke the truth — this spear will make
Whoever holds it stay awake.

'The tip must touch your head, that's all:
You'll find your eyelids never fall,
Not even if you have to hear
A teacher droning in your ear,
A party speech, a boring sermon,
Or seven operas in German.'

'Okay,' said Finn, 'I hope it's true,
Or else I'll stick this spear in *you*
And grill you on a barbecue!'

WAITING FOR MIDNIGHT

So back he ran with spear in hand,
Back to the feasting warrior band.
But now he found they all appeared
Much gloomier, as midnight neared.
In fire-proof night-wear they were dressed:
They really didn't look their best!

Around the hall they stood or sat,
Too fearful now to even chat —

Though Goll saw Finn, and gave a sneer:
'You really think that fancy spear
Will help you fight this fellow's tricks?
He'll turn it into cocktail sticks
Or bend it like elastic, maybe,
While you lie sleeping like a baby!'

The King said: 'Finn must do his best,
And we shall put him to the test —
If he succeeds, it's our good luck.'
And at that moment, midnight struck!

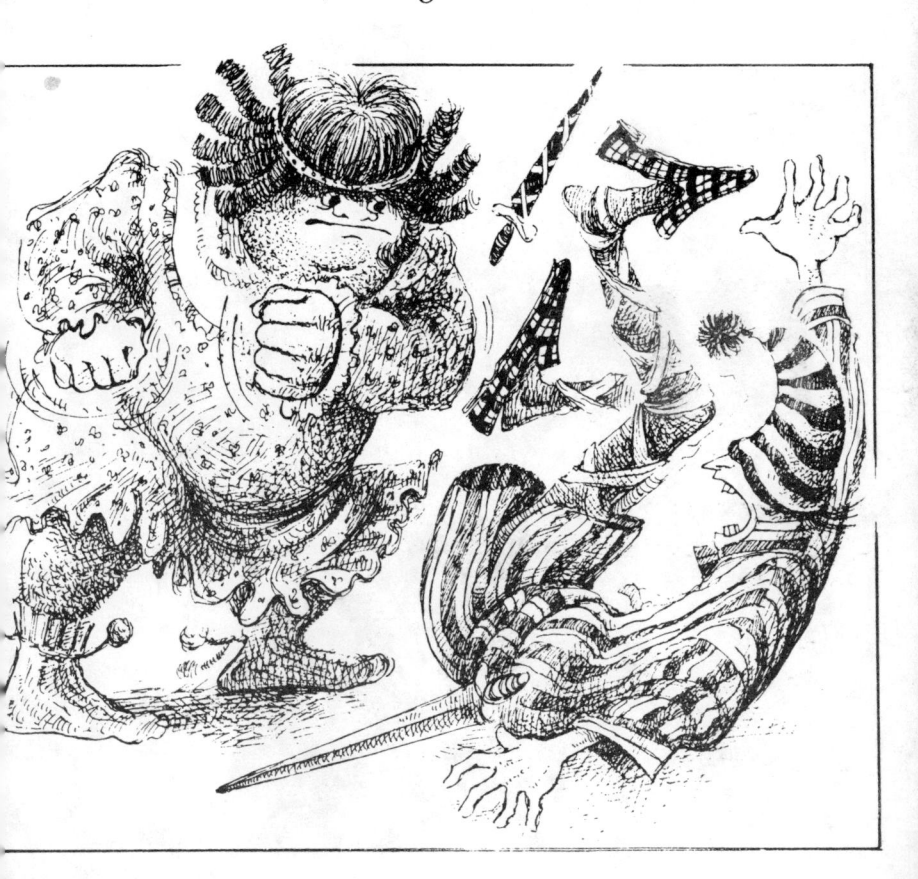

THE FIEND ARRIVES

They heard a sudden clap of thunder
That nearly split the roof asunder —
There was a bright blue blinding flash,
The doors flew open with a crash,
And there stood Aillen, ten feet tall.
He smiled and said: 'Good evening all!
You're welcome to my Late Late Show.
Sing hi-di-hi and ho-di-ho!
With Aillen you
   can have a ball —
The sharpest harpist
   of them all!'

The King said: 'Don't you ever tire
Of setting Tara's Hall on fire
And leaving all the people snoring?'

The Fiend said: 'No, it's never boring
To exercise my magic arts:
My fairy music tops the charts!'

'This building's priceless!' said the King.
'Doesn't tradition mean a thing?
We've tried to save it for the nation
By listing it for preservation.
Tonight, perhaps, the flames won't catch,
And you will find you've met your match!'

The Fire-Fiend scorned the High King's warning;
He said: 'You'll find, tomorrow morning,
I've burned your hall right to the ground.
And now, I'll make the music sound!'

THE MAGIC MUSIC

He plucked the strings, and then and there,
Enchanted music filled the air,
And soon the Fianna's eyes were closing
And every one of them was dozing.

Goll crashed at once upon the floor —
His snores were like a lion's roar,
One warrior felt his eyelids droop,
And fell face forward in the soup;
Others collapsed in one great heap,
And all of them were fast asleep.

But as the warriors slumped in slumber,
Brave Finn was not among their number,
For when the music reached his ear,
He leaned his head against the spear.
His snores and snuffles were a fake,
For really he was wide awake!

When Aillen saw the snoozing throng
He said: 'That didn't take too long —
And now I'll have my little joke,
And send the building up in smoke!'

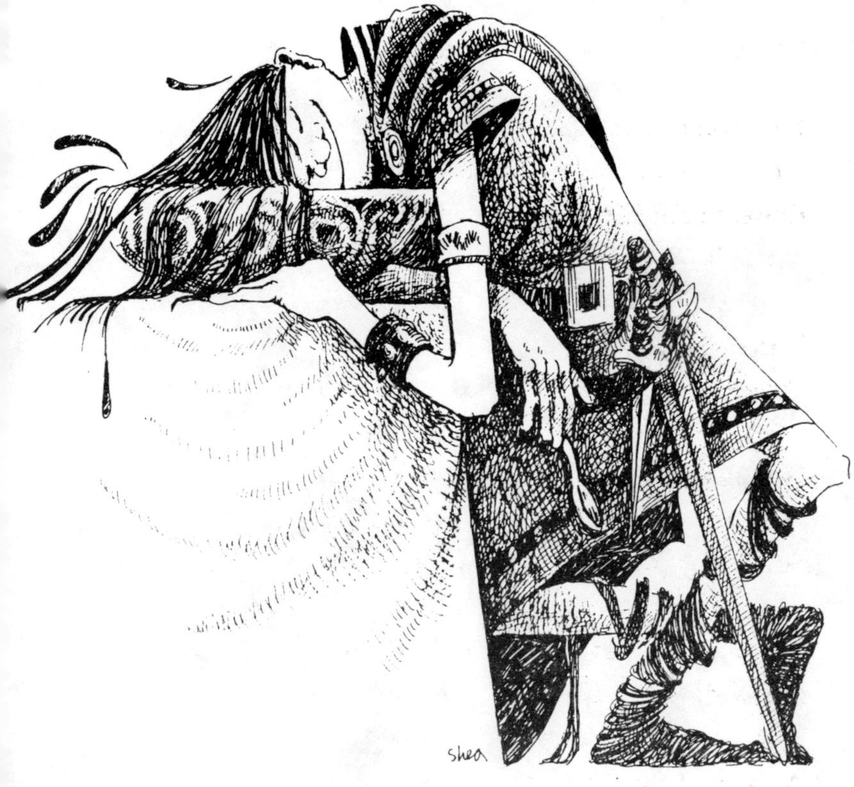

FINN'S ATTACK

He rushed outside — Finn followed after;
The Fiend gave out a roar of laughter,
And from his open mouth there came
A sizzling stream of fiery flame!

It roared like some great blazing torch,
Ready to singe and burn and scorch,
But Finn leaped out and shouted: 'Stay!
Mac Cool is here to save the day.
This is your final escapade,
For I am Finn, the Fire Brigade!'

The Fire-Fiend breathed out fire and smoke,
But Finn held up his crimson cloak:
It caught the flames and wrapped them round
And sent them down into the ground.
A mole said: 'Wow! This place is warm —
Who needs to go to Benidorm?'

The Fiend was looking grim as death,
And getting very out of breath.
He breathed one final blazing jet —
Finn's cloak just trapped it, like a net,
And sent it downwards with a sizzle.
The panting Fiend began to grizzle:

'You've won this time, but wait and see —
You haven't heard the last of me!'

'Oh yes, we have!' Finn raised his spear;
The Fiend fled, faster than a deer,
Into the dark and gloomy night.
Finn followed like a bird in flight,
Until he saw the Fire-Fiend stop
High up, upon a mountain-top.

Finn flung his spear, just like a dart —
It pierced the Fire-Fiend through the heart
And down he fell, extremely dead.
Then neatly, Finn chopped off his head
And took it back with cheerful glee
For all the warriors to see;
And when they opened up their eyes,
He'd give them all a nice surprise!

THE HERO

Night faded and the
  bright dawn broke,
And one by one,
  the warriors woke.
The King said:
  'Well, upon my soul!
Whatever's that,
  up on the pole?'

Finn bowed and smiled and calmly said:
'My Lord, it is the Fire-Fiend's head,
And I've got rid of him for good,
Just as I always said I would.'

Oh, how they cheered and stamped their feet!
It really was a lovely treat
To wake inside the feasting-hall
And find it wasn't burned at all.

The King said, when they'd all applauded:
'Our hero, Finn, must be rewarded.
Alone he bravely won the battle —
He'll have a hundred head of cattle,
And golden spoons, and silver bowls,
A year's supply of sausage rolls —
But best of all, I now decree,
The Fianna's leader he shall be!'

GOLL SULKS

The warrior band all cheered the choice —
But one refused to raise his voice:
Goll's joyfulness was not abundant,
For he had just been made redundant!

His hairy features sneered and scowled;
With rumbling rage he grimly growled.

The King said: 'Goll, your burly bulk
Looks very silly when you sulk.
Your firm allegiance you must vow,
For Finn will be your leader now.'

A silence fell: would Goll refuse
To let Finn step into his shoes?

Goll stood there, shaking like a jelly,
With twitching head and wobbling belly.

He gave a belch, a grunt, a groan,
Bit off a chunk of bison-bone
And spat it out upon the floor.
He strode away, and at the door
He turned and snarled: 'Goll never cringes!'
And tore the door right off its hinges.

The King said: 'Goll, I see you're cross —
But I've decided Finn's the Boss,
And I can tell you to be loyal,
For when all's said and done, I'm royal!'

They waited for a little while,
And then Goll gave a grisly smile.
He muttered: 'Now you've shown me, Finn —
The best man doesn't always win.'

LEADER OF THE FIANNA

He took Finn's hand and squeezed it hard,
As if it was a lump of lard.
Finn winced a bit, but told him: 'Thanks —
I'm glad to have you in the ranks.'

So Finn became, in one fell swoop,
The leader of that gallant troop.
The High King said: 'We'll feast tonight,
And honour Finn, with great delight.
I'll just say one thing, if I might —
Please, do not set the place alight!'

So Finn had kept his golden rule,
And earned his name — The Cool Mac Cool.